OUR PLANET
OUR FUTURE

CARING FOR THE FORESTS

Written by
Azra Limbada

BookLife
PUBLISHING

©2020
BookLife Publishing Ltd.
King's Lynn
Norfolk PE30 4LS

All rights reserved.
Printed in Malaysia.

A catalogue record for this
book is available from the
British Library.

ISBN: 978-1-83927-255-4

Written by:
Azra Limbada

Edited by:
John Wood

Designed by:
Drue Rintoul

PHOTO CREDITS

Images are courtesy of Shutterstock.com. With thanks to Getty Images, Thinkstock Photo and iStockphoto. Cover - Jackal Yu, zlikovec. 4&5 - Denis Tabler, Dudarev Mikhail. 6&7 - Smileus, Fotos593. 8&9 - Monkey Business Images, atiger. 10&11 - Papa Bravo, Tilo G. 12&13 - ALPA PROD, Thep Photos, Tyler Olson. 14&15 - Jay Ondreicka, Sumala Chidchoi. 16&17 - Peter J. Wilson, Soloviova Liudmyla. 18&19 - Rasta777, ZayacSK. 20&21 - Mike Jett. 22&23 - Pong Danviboon, Butsaya, Liz Kcer, kozirsky, Andrey Solovev, ConstantinosZ.

CONTENTS

Words that look like <u>this</u> can be found in the glossary on page 24.

EARTH

We live on Earth. Our planet is about 4.5 billion years old. It is home to all sorts of living things. Life can be found everywhere, from steamy jungles to dry deserts.

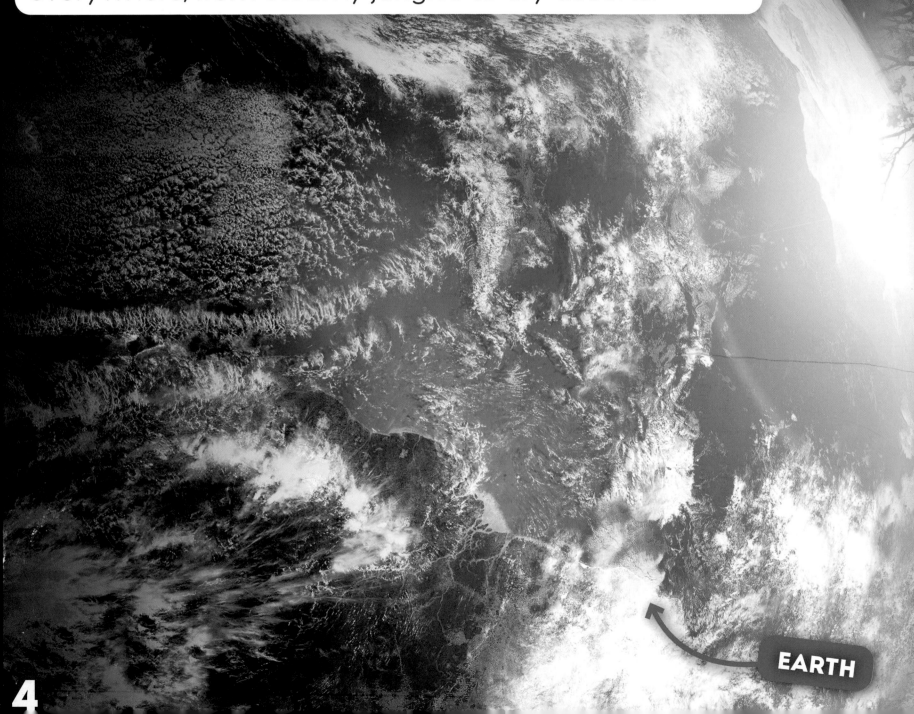

EARTH

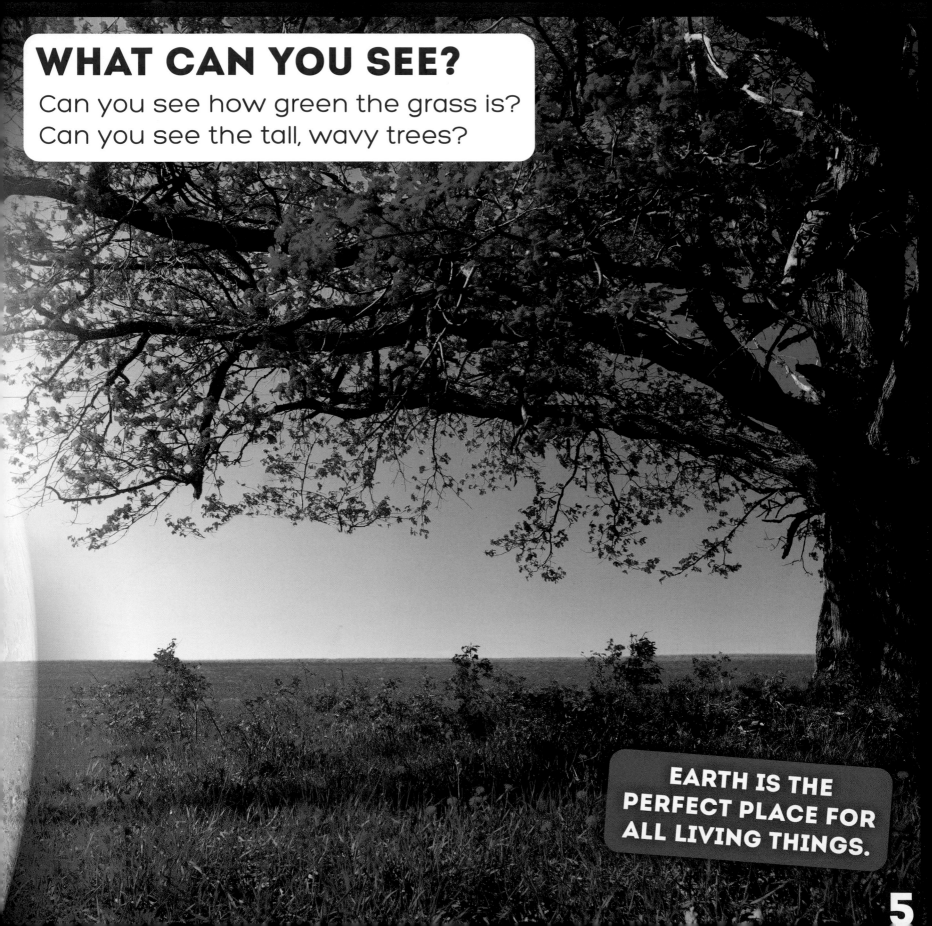

WHAT CAN YOU SEE?

Can you see how green the grass is?
Can you see the tall, wavy trees?

EARTH IS THE PERFECT PLACE FOR ALL LIVING THINGS.

FORESTS

A forest is made up of lots of different trees. Many animals live in forests and need them in order to stay alive.

WOODS ARE OFTEN SMALLER THAN FORESTS.

The Amazon is the largest rainforest in the world. A rainforest has lots of rain every year. There are millions of different <u>species</u> living in the Amazon.

OXYGEN AND CARBON DIOXIDE

Oxygen is all around us. It is a colourless <u>gas</u> that we need to stay alive. Every time we breathe in, we are taking in oxygen. Plants and trees make oxygen.

ALMOST ALL LIVING THINGS NEED OXYGEN.

Carbon dioxide is in the air that we breathe out. Trees and plants need carbon dioxide to grow. This means animals and plants <u>rely</u> on each other.

OXYGEN

CARBON DIOXIDE

WE NEED THE TREES AND THEY NEED US!

9

LIVING IN THE FOREST

Did you know that lots of people live in forests too? These people rely on trees and forests for their food and shelter.

MANY PEOPLE WHO LIVE IN THE RAINFORESTS ARE INVOLVED IN TRYING TO PROTECT THEM.

Animals also need the forest to live. Animals such as sloths and monkeys use tall trees for shelter and to hide from their <u>predators</u>.

SLOTH

DEFORESTATION

Deforestation is when trees in forests are cut down. Cutting down trees without planting new ones is bad for the <u>environment</u>.

DEFORESTATION ALSO MEANS THAT ANIMAL <u>HABITATS</u> ARE DESTROYED.

ONE WAY THAT YOU CAN HELP IS BY PLANTING TREES.

You can help stop deforestation by being responsible and reusing things that are made from trees, such as paper and card.

15

FOREST FIRES

A forest fire might be started by something in nature, such as a lightning strike. However, most forest fires are caused by humans.

Forest fires destroy habitats and add to the <u>pollution</u> around us. Sadly, it often takes a long time for a forest to recover from a fire.

FOREST FIRES ARE OFTEN CAUSED BY CAMPFIRES. REMEMBER TO ALWAYS BE SAFE WITH YOUR CAMPFIRE!

MINING

Mining is when humans dig deep into the ground to get things such as metals and coal. Coal is used to make electricity, but it causes lots of pollution.

Lots of trees are cut down before mining can happen. Mining can also pollute the ground or water nearby, killing even more plants and trees.

ISRA HIRSI

This is Isra Hirsi. She is an <u>activist</u> who is trying to stop <u>climate change</u>. Isra wants everyone to work together to help protect our planet.

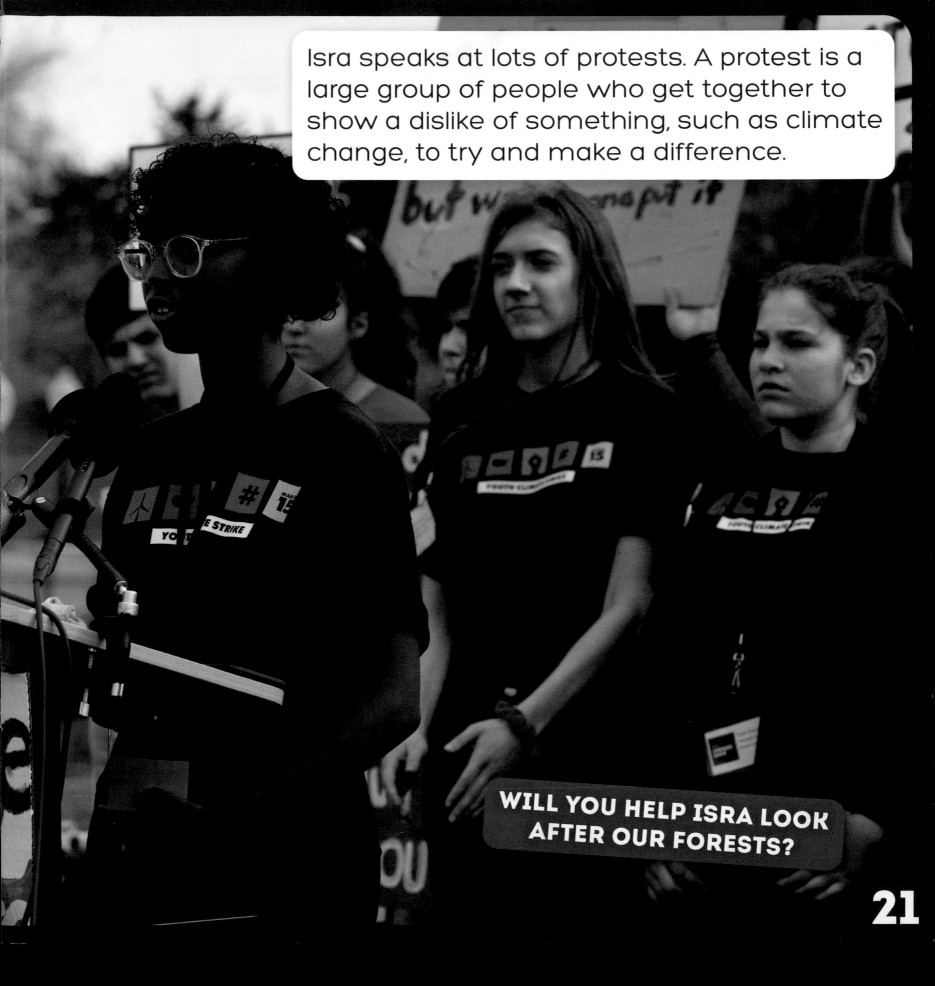

Isra speaks at lots of protests. A protest is a large group of people who get together to show a dislike of something, such as climate change, to try and make a difference.

WILL YOU HELP ISRA LOOK AFTER OUR FORESTS?

21

MAKE YOUR OWN RECYCLED WIND CHIMES

Here's everything you need to make your own recycled wind chimes.

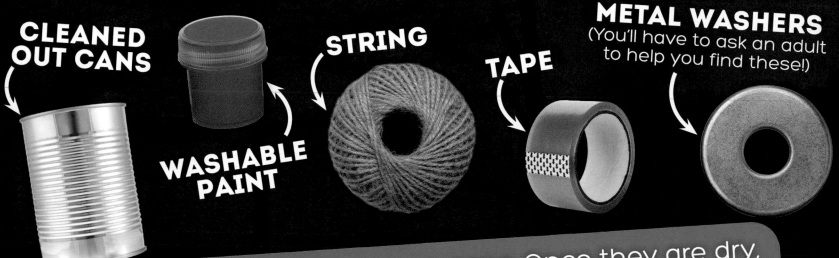

CLEANED OUT CANS

WASHABLE PAINT

STRING

TAPE

METAL WASHERS
(You'll have to ask an adult to help you find these!)

STEP 1: Paint the outside of your cans. Once they are dry, ask an adult to make a hole in the bottom of the cans.

STEP 2: Push your string through the hole.

STEP 3: Tie some washers along one end of the string, inside the cans. They will hold the string in place and make noise.

STEP 4: Hang the cans outside using tape. When the wind blows, they will make a lovely sound.

GLOSSARY

activist	someone who tries to make a change by speaking out
climate change	a change in the typical weather or temperature of a large area
environment	the natural world
gas	a thing that is like air, which spreads out to fill any space available
habitats	the natural homes in which animals, plants and other living things live
pollution	when something is added to our environment that is harmful to living things
predators	animals that hunt other animals for food
recycle	use again to make something else
rely	trust or depend on something
species	a group of very similar animals or plants that can create young together

INDEX